OVERCOMING DISTRACTIONS WHILE BUILDING SOMETHING GREAT

Aaron J. Mobley, Jr.

Aaron J. Mobley, Jr.

DEDICATION

Building while facing adversity can be one of the hardest tasks an individual will ever experience, but the joys of seeing a vision fulfilled is well worth the work. I want to dedicate this book to every individual who has made the decision to continue building through life's often precarious circumstances. Your strength is an example of just how great your dream really is.

Aaron J. Mobley, Jr.

TABLE OF CONTENTS

Let's get started!

LIVING ON TARGET

How would you feel if you didn't discover what you wanted to do in life until it was time for you to die? I know it's a morbid way to think, but would you instead think about it now when you have time to change or then when it'll probably be too late. It's a sad reality that many individuals experience as they live for the dreams and hopes of others while neglecting and silencing what's important to them. It's entirely possible to help others and stay focused on your life's direction at the same time. It only takes a strong will and an adamant desire to live full of purpose and destiny. Oh yeah, it's going to require some intentional efforts towards setting priorities that are flexible to sudden change or transition.

All of us in a fairytale world should be able to set a plan and see it come to an end without anything happening in the middle. But all of us know that this is rarely the story when building something great. It kind of seems like as long as you were creating mediocre things that everything flowed effortlessly. All the resources you needed were there, all the people to support it was in place, and nothing came even to attempt to stop you.

The truth of the matter is that certain things come to disrupt the market. These are innovative ideas that have the potential to revolutionize an industry or a particular way of thought. Whenever you intend to build anything like this, you should be prepared to focus and sometimes fight.

Setting priorities based on the portion of building you are in will help you move through some of these challenges. Knowing where and whom to give your attention to is one of the things that often delay the final product from being displayed. It's hard to provide everything to everything or everyone when you are building change, and one of the greatest mistakes you can have is feeling guilty because of it.

Priorities help you manage life as it changes at a moment's notice. It makes you aware of what time, energy, and resources you must give to a particular area during that space of time. Individuals that don't place order in their lives often live by the illusion that they have more than they do. I'm just not speaking of financially; I'm more so speaking of internal energy. Have you ever just run out of gas internally? You've got the people-power and the financial means to make it happen, but you just didn't have the momentum within to continue building. The foundation is strong. The structure looks great, but you don't have the personal passion needed to finish what you started. Well, throughout this book, I desire to help you regain the passion for what you've created and even the passion for beginning what you never thought you could.

DON'T WASTE YOUR TIME
Maximize Your Moments

Have you ever heard these saying, "Time is gold" or "Time waits for no man"? Doesn't it seem like the more time we need, the more time we lose sometimes? This further promotes the fact

11

that setting priorities professionally and personally is one of the primary keys to your future success. There are no real disadvantages to placing things in order in your life. The only results are a well-managed life that will promote structure and growth.

Let's look at the gardener and his garden. He chooses the right area to cultivate the soil with plans to plant seeds. Now it might take some time, but he waits patiently, knowing that those seeds will produce a beautiful display of flowers one day if given the right nourishment. The flowers grow and grow. Some of the bushes that are connected to it grow as well. But the gardener has a particular shape in mind, and the once tamed display is now growing wild. So, what does the gardener do? Does he just allow all his work to go untamed and unmanaged? No. He takes pruning shears and begins to bring control to his still beautiful display.

Sometimes in life, it will take you remembering your investment and the time it took to get where you are. It was your time, sweat, and tears that produced what you are now seeing as your most significant accomplishment, and no one should have the right to take it away.

Time is one of the only things that continue moving without ever significantly going back. The one time a year that time goes back, it only stays that way until it's time to move forward again. The years will continue to go by, and you are honestly getting no younger.

You never seem to get enough time. Even if you are given forty hours in a day, you still won't be able to get enough of it. Somehow, some things will come up, and you will end up wanting more time. Time is a precious commodity. Once it's gone, it can't be recovered.

The fact is: when you are busy working on goals, time flies swiftly. But when you are not, time seems to be at a standstill. This is the cause of much of our frustrations. Our lack of setting priorities and maximizing the time we are given will often cause us to be overly irritated at our present circumstances because we seemingly can't do anything about them. We're just basically in a perpetual pause. Every day seems like it is just like the one before it.

Let's see if we can get that cycle to change for you by providing you with a few practical keys to help you maximize your time:

1. **Review your schedule at the start of the day.** Go over it in its entirety. You may notice that portions of your day may be crowded or hectic while some may not be too frenzied. Distribute your activities evenly throughout the day. This will help you not to feel rushed or overwhelmed.

Keep notepads handy so that you can keep track of your schedule. It also helps to remind you of your tasks and commitments. Notepads and schedule notebooks help you avoid overlapping of activities. In the case of overlaps, determine which one is a priority. This will be easy if you are techy because you can download an app or use the reminder or note option already loaded on your device.

After spreading your schedule for the day and still feeling overwhelmed by the number of tasks to be accomplished, you may have to forego some of them by re-scheduling the other tasks for another day. It's not that you are procrastinating. It's just that you understand that certain things can wait for you to accomplish goals as priorities and still have a peaceful disposition.

What you are doing is very much like cleaning your house. When your home is in order, you avoid running into misplaced furniture, opening closets that are filled to the brim, and accidentally getting knocked on the head by falling objects every time you open the door. Also, if it is in order, you will likely find spare spaces available. This is precisely what you need to grow your dream or vision. MORE SPACE!

Here's a bonus point. It's not fair or kind to throw others into your emergency or rushed situations because you haven't learned how to manage your time well. They will feel the anxious energy you produce, and it might cause them not to be as accommodating to you in the future. Allow others to experience the joys of the time they spend with you and not just the sorrows produced from the time you wasted.

2. **Don't wait until the last minute to announce changes.** If you are meeting with someone or can't make an appointment, request a reschedule in advance. The truth is that some meetings are destiny related, and I suppose that it is a good idea to see every appointment like that. You just never know who has been called to help you get to your next place of opportunity.

One of the principles that advance life is the principle of honor. Honor not only promotes you, but it also promotes the value that you place on others. Valuing another person's time will demonstrate something compelling to them. It's an automatic plus when you are an individual that arrives on-time or early and is conscientious of another person's time if a cancellation is necessary.

3. **You're already a creative genius.** Use your creativity to bring time to life. For example, you need to do the laundry, but at the same time, you also must rush and buy some groceries. Perhaps, what you can do is to set your washing machine to do the laundry while you step out to the grocers. Manage your time in the grocery and back home, just in time when the laundry is done.

You can even do the cooking simultaneously by using a slow cooker (I make the best crockpot mac and cheese, by the way). It cooks food by itself. You can even pick up the kids from school after shopping. Four tasks are combined into one. All it takes is scheduling and a little creativity. Learning to multitask while remaining efficient is a key that you will use in more places than one. Make it a habit, and you'll see growth in every area of your life.

4. **You're not a superhero.** When you have to do a specific task for the first time, it is natural to have mistakes. However, a first-time task doesn't have to be a disaster. If there is no clear direction on how things should be done, take the time to plan it out before you act. This saves time, energy, and money. I have two favorite words that I frequently use when setting goals and projections. Those words are PLAN and PREPARE. I often find that much of the frustration that comes while building greatness only arrives because of the lack of planning and preparation. Anything that you deem as great should be prepared for and given the necessary amount of time to develop behind the scenes before you try to execute it personally.

5. **Meditate.** There's a definition connected to the word meditate that I love. It says that to meditate is to form the image within

yourself. With every goal and dream you have, it's always good to sit with yourself. Meditating before executing a plan will help you see any needed precautions, any difficulties that might arise, and any areas that can be expanded.

Visualize the possible outcome of your plan. Seek out other ways of getting it accomplished and then choose the best of those options. Remember, options give you power. Having the right to control the variables in your plan will motivate confidence in you as you build. If there is only one option, do it just the same. Some tasks may appear complicated when you think about it, but not necessarily when put into action.

You will never have enough time, but you can make it work for you when you choose to maximize every moment you are given. You deserve this moment. Elect to make the best of it by developing a plan to make it work for you.

Aaron J. Mobley, Jr.

A KILLER COUPLE:
Regret and Resentment

Regret is a terrible monster. It will eat at your present existence like the craziest strain of bacteria and won't rest until your future is entirely consumed. Regret is a constant reminder of every missed opportunity and door that you chose not to walk through or might not have had the chance to at that moment. If we think about it, some of the things that disappoint us about the past are things that we had no other option in. We were born in that family and provided with limited resources to accomplish goals at that time. So, it's not regretting ourselves; sometimes, it's regretting not being in control of the variables surrounding our lives.

I remember a story that my wife shared with me concerning a co-worker's daughter. She went into the store with her mother, who was currently raising her alone. The daughter wanted something expensive, and the mother, aware of her financial means, said, "No." The daughter, in anger and disappointment, yells out, "Why did I have to be born into a poor family?" While this might sound to some like a humorous story, it's often what causes many adults to be regretful. It's kind of like we have been robbed of something. We think that if the variables were different, we would've had it. But guess what? There's nothing that you can change about things that occurred before your birth, during your childhood, or any time where you were not in control of how events played out. It's going to be up to you to accept and believe that. Now, how you proceed from that point on is totally up to you.

One of the biggest obstacles in becoming successful is most certainly past regrets. We get so caught up on what could've been that we become stalkers to it and cannot accomplish anything without looking in the mirror at what we view as the ones that got away.

What happens is that you now program your mind to fail. You set a schedule in your heart for the disappointment that hasn't even shown up and might never arrive if you hadn't created it. Most of the failures we experience are linked to the past. We create what is still a part of us in the present, and if regret is still a part of your heart, you will often attempt to recreate the same situation as the one you missed out on.

Attempting to recreate past situations is a disaster waiting to happen. Why is this? Because time has changed the variables. Nothing is as it was. You've grown, life's surroundings have changed, and hopefully, you are much wiser. These types of replay situations will end most of the time the same way. You arrive at the conclusion that I never should've tried that again. What past situations are you attempting to recreate? Is it the rekindling of a past relationship? Restarting an old business? Or going back to get the degree in that subject that you didn't want anyway?

One of the best ways to release the hold that regret has on you is to accept that you are and have always been human. This gives you a natural right not to be perfect at everything and during every situation. But through every situation, you also have the human ability to learn from them and better situations in the future.

A DISASTROUS COUPLE

Most people who live in regret also have regrets lifelong partner who is resentment. Not only are you regretting not taking advantage of previous opportunities, but you are even now resenting the people and things you sacrificed them for. I wonder how many people are living through your sudden mood swings and have no idea why? Sometimes they even gave you the option not to sacrifice for them, and you did it anyway with the positive outlook that it would work out wonderfully. When it doesn't, it becomes an issue for you and everyone else around you. They now have to pay the price for my disappointment because the truth is that if it wasn't for the decision I made for them, I would not be experiencing this (that's exactly what we think sometimes). But what if I told you that you might've still experienced it? Would it make it better in your head? Would your outlook towards those around you change?

You still would have had to take certain routes no matter who was involved, where you went, and what options you chose. It was your path, and regardless of your decisions, it would be your journey to take.

What's interesting about regret is that it's often one-sided. No one knows how things would've turned out on the other side or whether you would've been happier than you are at this current time in your life. I suppose that it's just the idea that another option looks better than the circumstances that you are looking at on the surface right now. Regret feeds you with enough information to keep you stuck. It doesn't want you to see beyond it. It will help you find reasons to be resentful through television shows, the accomplishments of others, your children's success, and more.

Have you ever just not been happy for someone else? You don't have to admit it openly, but there are times when building that you are tired of seeing the fast construction of another person's dreams. Within yourself, you know that it wasn't as fast as it looks, but it also appears that your dream is taking a much slower pace than you would've liked. The lack of happiness for others goes far beyond jealousy. It's rooted in regret and resentment.

This is something that I've come to believe and honestly understand. I think that we all make the best decisions that we can when we must make them. I choose not to think that anyone just willingly decides to do something they know will turn out terribly. Some choices are just made because of the lack of additional information or the feeling that there are no other options. Unfortunately, these are sometimes the choices that you can live with now but might kill you down the road.

One of the most incredible levels of personal victory you can gain in life is power OVER regret. You'll never be able to travel back in time to get that college degree during your youth, but you can go back and get it now. You can't take back those poor financial choices that made you lose what was valuable to you, but you can make a concerted effort to be financially wise so that it doesn't happen again. The idea here is to understand what you are personally regretting and to use the information as fuel to gain wisdom in.

Learn to make decisions from where you are now and not from the point where you seemingly failed. I can almost guarantee you that even though you might've failed in your own eyes, there were lessons throughout the journey that you would've never learned.

PASSIONLESS PURPOSE
Avoiding running on empty

One of the ideas that I have been thinking about lately is how effective we are at being effective. It's kind of like we build a level of pride in the knowledge that no matter where we are or what we're given to do, we can make it happen. But let's look at this carefully because this can be a benefit as well as a disadvantage when the time comes for you to pursue your own life goals. Many of you reading this can probably go back through your life history and pinpoint instances where you were helping everyone else, taking care of someone else's vision, but the moment you attempted to take time out for yours, things began to get a little crazy. Not with the vision, but with the people that you were helping.

Let's place a pause here and jump on this soapbox. You must learn that even while you plan and project your vision forward, it's equally important to be cautious of where you spend your time, efforts, and energy in the interim. No, you may not be starting that business today or going back for that degree tomorrow, but you also don't want to waste time in a place where you are not receiving an investment. Your in-between places must be places where you are learning and gaining momentum for your next advance. The people that you assist while building must also be those that will freely release and support you as you move forward.

One of the most inopportune moments any person can experience is to give everything to someone else's efforts and not see the support return when you finally stand on your own. Have you ever thought to yourself during situations like this whether those people ever wanted you to grow beyond them?

Unfortunately, life is filled with individuals who take pleasure in keeping you limited. Sometimes, we waste time in unproductive places and with unproductive people because we can't do what you're passionate about at the moment. Find something that you can use as a foundation, building block, or launchpad. Now that I've gotten that out let's continue!

What I have discovered is that people love what you do. Especially if you do it well, if it's going to help them or advance what they're involved in, they will "love the passion for your purpose right out of you." I know that sounds crazy but let me tell you what I mean. We are often restricted to exploring other areas of success, not because we don't have potential but because we are so good at not using it. Can you imagine the different areas of your gifts that have yet to be discovered and how much MORE successful you could be if you had the freedom and support to do so? So, what's stopping you? What's hindering you from trying something new or pursuing what you really love?

Honestly, you probably make a lot of money doing things for people that you could do with your eyes closed. It is not because you love doing it, but there's a demand for it, and you might be the only one who knows how to get it done. Someone might say, "Well, isn't that what you would call a dream job?" It may be, but to others who have a desire to build something greater for themselves, it's not. What ends up happening is that it takes up all your time and energy, and the thing that you have a passion for slowly dies out because you are consumed with accommodating others' needs.

People will always love you for what you have to offer and will hold you hostage to your areas of success. You are great at it. This is what blocks those watching you from understanding what you want to change anything. They'll sit you down and tell you why it's a terrible idea. All of which are most likely based on success points that they can pick out from what you're currently involved in. Anyone can find a reason to move onto something else when it's going bad, but how do you convince people that you need a change when you're frankly doing GREAT?

One of the hardest things that you will ever have to get someone to understand is that what makes success important to you is when its related to your passion. When you can go to bed and look forward to doing it, it really makes you happy. When you are doing what you love, it's not work to you. It's LIFE! You honestly live through your passion, and everyone around you can see the difference in attitude and behavior because of it. If you ever want to see a cranky person, go find someone who is just working a job to pay the bills and has no passion, like or love for what they are doing. They'll make your life and dealings with them miserable.

Think about it. When you are working in your passion, it doesn't matter how many distractions come your way or how many roadblocks you have to overcome; you are okay with it and can ignore it and keep pushing without hesitation. I'm not saying that you won't have your days where you'll feel like giving up, but you don't because there's a greater purpose involved now. You're not just working anymore. The complete essence of what you have been designed to do is now being displayed. You do it because you love doing it even when the return doesn't seem as great during certain seasons.

I want to make something clear. It's great talking about pursuing passion and life-long dreams. Still, the reality is that for most of us, there will be seasons where we have to be disconnected from passion externally while we are taking care of the business of life to keep things stable in our personal worlds. But the thought is always to keep what's passionate to you are a THOUGHT. There's a powerful scripture that ends like this, "...As a man thinketh so is he". There have never been so truer words spoken. Even if you can't do it now, never forget the power of what it means to you. You pursuing your dreams means something to YOU. Whether it means something to others, it does to you, and you'll never know what fruitfulness can come of your life if you don't remember it.

Don't ever allow your dreams and visions to go downstream, never to be seen again, because you are caught up on life and the circumstances that have caused you to let them go. Life has a way of getting out of hand, you know. One event after another, and now you're watching the years go by, and you don't know how to get them back if you tried. Don't let this happen to you. You've got so much more to offer the world around you.

Discover ways to stay connected to your passion while purpose develops. There is a day of opportunity coming where you'll get paid for doing what you love to do and not what you have to do.

IT'S JUST NOT THERE ANYMORE

What do you do when you have lost your passion in an area where you have been successful and are probably still successful? This is where it gets a little tricky. You're still making money doing it. People are still coming for it, but you just don't enjoy it anymore. I've certainly been in that position a time or two in my life. Every time I start to feel this way, I must ask myself a few questions:

- Am I just feeling this way because something isn't working the way I want?
- Is this something that I was really called to do?
- Have I ever really been passionate about it?
- Am I just doing this because it's what people expect me to do?
- What would happen if I decided to do something different?

Sadly, many people will continue doing what they don't enjoy because of the benefit that it provides to others. They will take themselves totally out of the equation without understanding that your purpose should be at most times mutually benefiting. That means that as much as you like doing it, something should be returned to you in some fashion or form. Some people just love cooking. They love picking out the right ingredients. They will plant vegetables and fruits ahead of time just to have them ready for that special meal. They literally enjoy the process that it takes to prepare every stage of the meal. But what's amazing is that for all the work that was involved, they get most of their pleasure from watching others enjoy what they have done.

You have probably heard countless stories of individuals who didn't go to school or who may have never moved away because of how it would affect others. You probably also know the regret they have for not taking advantage of the same opportunity. It's a difficult task to handle sometimes when life provides doors. Do I go? Or Do I stay? Are often the only questions you ask yourself. Let's look a little further. I'm curious as to which side of the fence you'll be on after reading this.

The idea of Living on Target is being totally okay with making choices that are the best for you as being inspired by a greater source within you. There must be a greater call heard within you. Finding out what's sourcing your ability to move toward something will help you qualify its standing in your life. Every move we make is sourced by some sort of energy. Whether you're doing it because you must or want to it's still being confirmed by something within you.

So, what's driving your decision? The answer to that question might startle some of us because we know that most of our decisions are fueled by the feeling that we have a lack of options, hopelessness or emergency situations that have to be settled at a moment's notice. Any decision made from any of those places have a proven track record in leading to directly into regret and resentment. The truth is that you're going to have to find a way to be content while you make hard decisions that might make you uncomfortable. You might not be able to spend as much as you have in past seasons, or you might not be able to socialize like you've done before. The idea is that it's okay with making decisions that make you hurt if they are going to make you happy. I laughed as I was typing that because it sounds crazy, but it's true.

Let's take for an example, the idea of working towards being fit. You already have in your mind the goal you want to reach, but it will take you not eating certain things and working out physically. You haven't worked out in years. During that first training session, it might hurt. But most certainly, the day after, effects will be much worse. You continue to do it why? Because it will make you happy in the end.

The process towards living a life filled with passion isn't always pretty. In some seasons, it is downright ugly and seemingly disastrous, but the end is so beautiful if you learn to stay focused.

LEARNING A NEW VOICE

From this point on you have to make the choice never to allow any temporary situation to force you to make a permanent decision. I know that this is a popular theme today, but it still rings so true.

There's a greater source of direction that is tugging at your heart and mind now. You've seen the best and worst of times and are conditioned to sacrifice to build what you have only imagined. Despite what anyone sees or thinks they know. You know that there is a greater pull working within your current decision. That power is GOD. FOLLOW GOD!

Have you ever considered that just maybe God is tugging at the way you believe or what you thought was important? Just maybe it's your true destiny that's calling you and you're not able to hear it clearly because you've never really listened to it before. That's one of the scariest thoughts ever right?

I recently watched a video of a baby who was born deaf get a hearing implant turned on. The excitement and joy on his face when he heard his parent's voice for the first time. I'm sure he couldn't understand the words or what they were saying, but he was for the first time hearing their voices. How would that feel to you to hear God's voice in vision for the first time?

I've got a question for you. So, if I haven't been listening to the God in you then who and what have you been listening to. Don't worry. I'll help you answer it. It's been the god outside of you. The god called people. The god called circumstances. The god called trouble, and the list goes on and on. The sound of being led by any of those things just seems so awful, but it's whom we listen to in most circumstances. I want this day to be different from the others that you've seen, but it's going to take TRUST.

1. Trusting in what is divine for you.
2. Trusting in what is authentic to you.
3. Trusting in what is passion to you.

If you're saying, yes, that's me, please understand that you're not the only one who is having to learn a new voice. We are all becoming acquainted with a new way of seeing ourselves in a new place and in a new time. Moving from one place to another is an exciting idea, but it takes work. Learning new surroundings, modes of travel and environments take time. Don't panic if you get uncomfortable. Your inconvenience now is going to pay off royally if you just stick with the plan and follow what you hear clearly and identify it without a doubt as God. Remember this as you share your visions for the future with others. Your God may not be theirs. That list we went over earlier might be the idol that other individuals in your life are still listening to. You must learn to evaluate the "push back" you get from others during these times. Why are they against this idea? What do they think will happen? Why can't they see this as God?

Many times, they can't see it because it's foreign to them. It's not a language that they recognize. So, you really expect someone who has never ventured out to do anything or wanted to do anything to understand this skyscraper of a plan that you've come up with? And to be honest, it might not even be intentional. Sometimes it's just because they can't understand the language or the idea that fear is never a good reason not to try something. Here's a few more reasons why you might be experiencing opposition to your vision:

- They've tried it, and it didn't work for them.
- They want you to stay on their level.
- They're afraid to try new things.
- They know that they're not called to do it anyway.

There's many more, but if you are going to build something great you are going to have to acquaint yourself with the tools that others might use against your accomplishments and achievements.

Lastly, it's a common occurrence to be more trusting in everyone else but discredit the power of your own voice. You should probably make a list of things and people that made you "dumb". Things that stopped you from speaking your truth or took away the power you had to speak. All of us can probably think of situations where we felt helpless and afraid. After making that list, I want you to remember and then forget.

I want you to remember only with the hopes that you'll never allow those things, circumstances, or people to steal your voice again. I want you to forget because to move forward you'll have to erase the stigma it created in your life. The scars that sometimes go so deep that any form of challenge will cause you to stop in your tracks only to relive the pain all over again. Get your voice back. Talk up! Clear your throat and announce what is important to you. If people don't get it at first or never get it, it's okay.

Understanding that your voice matters will give you the strength to speak more clearly, loudly, and forcibly. You deserve to be heard. Your wants deserve to be fulfilled. You have a right to live in your greatest moment.

Aaron J. Mobley, Jr.

GETTING OFF THE ROAD TO NOWHERE

ave you ever thought that maybe you're on this constant cycle that might lead you nowhere? Often, it's because you are really living "off target". What this means is that most likely you're just taking it one day at a time. While this sounds like the best you can do, there are other things that you can do to ensure that as you're managing life's circumstances, you're also setting goals and going after your dreams.

Living off target also has a lot to do with what you're currently pursuing. Sometimes we are honestly pursuing things that we literally have no interest in. Isn't it funny how you can spend tens of thousands of dollars going to school only to get a degree that you really don't want? Get a job that you have no interest in only to work for years in something that never really fulfilled you? All of those are the results of living off target.

It's so easy to get stuck while taking care of life's experiences. You really do need the money, so you do take the job. You really do need the support of your family and friends, so you move back to the place that you know is not good for your purpose. It makes perfect sense as a temporary fix, but it's important that you never forget your TRUE TARGET.

What are you doing to get back on course? What are the decisions that you are making today that will help you get back to the place you want to be in life or the place that you've only dreamed of? Don't get stuck in a place thinking that it's your permanent residence. You've got a whole lot of life yet to live and today is the start of something new. If you'll allow it.

SO, WHAT ABOUT THIS LIFE STUFF?

Life just happens you know. It just continues moving whether you're sitting still or whether it seems like you are traveling down the expressway. It doesn't matter what you're already dealing with it just comes. Truthfully, it happens to everyone. Unforeseen, unexpected and most of all unwanted experiences occur to us all. While some of us are more transparent when they do show up, believe me, it's more common than you think. The universe is not playing some sort of "She or He is my favorite victim" game. God is not selecting to place all the drama in your lap and let everyone else go by with a free pass. Everyone experiences something at one time or another. How you learn to manage it is going to be one of the greatest tasks you'll ever be given and one of the most significant lessons that you'll be taught. I want you to listen to this closely to what I'm about to say.

One of the first traveling lessons that I have learned and continue to learn is how to pack light. Packing light is a method that every marathon runner should be an expert in. The race is long. There are many miles ahead, and one of the most detrimental things to do is pack too heavily.

Sometimes in life before we can expend energy on our dreams, we get into this crazy idea that taking everything and everyone is necessary. We overload our schedules, lives, relationships and then try to take off. Guess what? Sometimes we never do. The idea of packing light is profound. Only taking the essentials on this new journey will help you move quicker while gaining more ground.

What's important to you in this season of your life? Who's necessary and beneficial to you as you purpose to move forward? These are the types of questions that you should ask yourself as you evaluate where you are and where you're going. There's really no time to waste. There's tons of work yet to be done.

4–KEYS TO GETTING OFF THE ROAD TO NOWHERE

1. **Understand the importance of preparation:** There is no such thing as

just showing up. If you are to meet any level of opportunity it must be after your intentional season of preparation. Many people live off the idea that something is just going to drop out of the sky and then they'll be set for the rest of their lives. Guess what? This is a rare occurrence. Let's say it does happen. What will help you maintain it and use it to advance is still going to be what you have prepared within and about yourself long before it ever showed up. **Preparation allows you to meet opportunity when it shows up!**

2. **Be properly positioned to pursue:** Have you ever tried to run after something on foot on concrete or a stony surface without shoes on? This is how some of us are when we attempt to go after our dreams. We're running but having to stop because of some sort of

damage because we refused to get positioned to pursue. This also has a lot to do with the position of your heart and your life. Making sure that you're emotionally clear will aide you in making the sound and necessary decisions for your future despite oppositions from individuals who might not understand.

3. **Keep your ears open:** From the day you receive your first idea until the day you create the next one, you'll constantly be hearing. Don't shut off the listening capability of your spirit after you begin seeing results. God wants to keep you sharp and ahead of the game. For this to happen you're going to have to listen more than you speak and be ready to implement change at a moment's notice if the wind changes. Don't get married to a method. Keep listening.

4. Act like you want it: So, you've got some great dreams and ideas, and you're pursuing them. The only problem is that you're not running like you're trying to win. What you have within you is worth the extra push. Don't give any room within yourself not to achieve. The prize of just running shouldn't be your highest achievement. You should want to win. After working so hard, you deserve to have exactly what you want and enjoy the benefits of it for years to come.

MAINTAINING MOMENTUM DURING UNCERTAIN TIMES

There is really not a 100% way to be absolutely certain about how life will choose to get you from A to B. The routes and modes of travel that destiny takes to get us to it are many times beyond what is rational or even explainable. Have you ever considered that just maybe there was a greater force that was drawing you like a man tied to another? Regardless of how you tugged and attempted to get away it was the path that was chosen for you and you had to do it that way.

Well, I want to announce that if that is what you were thinking you are right. As mighty and controlling as we can be sometimes destiny has its own creator, and that's God. Whatever you chose to think of him as that's exactly who's pulling the strings. It's funny how we assume that we are driving because we can go in certain directions at various times in our life. We are confident that we are the ones that are guiding our path or choosing what's best for us. But we're not.

There is something that cannot be denied within you working. It's a power greater than any adversity or challenge. Even in times where you seem helpless. You're not helpless at all. You've got the power to tap into a momentum that will lead you exactly where you need to be during every season of your life.

If you sit down and try to ponder on the vast understanding of your journeys in life, you might just burst. The complexities are so deep, wide, high, and long you'll never really be able to completely get it until you get to the end. The end of what you ask? The end of life. Life is a constantly evolving creature. It grows and grows, and we grow with it. Not only do we adapt, but we expand.

The idea we once had about certain areas of our life seemingly grows as our bodies do. In areas that we were limited we are now able to see another side that we refused to acknowledge. This idea here is to always know that whatever the route or avenue taken, you will eventually surround the thing that you are pursuing. That's a wonderful idea, isn't it? You're not only approaching it. You're surrounding it. The goal is not only going to be the finish line, but it's going to be the center. Why? Because every goal that is connected to your passion grows within you as you run after it.

TO FAR AHEAD TO TURN AROUND

I cannot count how many times I have gone after something and when it got a little rough wanted to turn around and choose something that seemed a little bit easier. Who willingly runs into danger or trouble with a smile anyway? I don't find too many people that will admit that there are times when the goal just doesn't seem worth it anymore. It's not that the value of the goal that has changed. It's that you are not finding the worth in achieving it.

Life provides so many options that convince us that some things aren't worth the trouble. We do it in relationships, professions, business connections and even where it concerns our passion. Often, we find ways to avoid what we see down the road as opposition and conclude a situation long before it ever occurring. Thus, robbing ourselves of the opportunity to see it never happen the way it has played out in our heads.

Isn't it funny to think that most of the reasons you came up with not to pursue your dreams weren't going to happen anyway? God had already devised a plan to get you to the end, and it wouldn't be as hard as you made it out to be.

Have you ever heard of someone getting to the last year of college and then just not having the drive to pursue it to the end? If you're not that person yourself. But what normally happened was the family and friends that supported that individual rallied around them to remind them concerning how far they had come.

Let's pause for a moment. You've got to have people around you that are absolutely invested in where you are going. Considering this thought, don't be mistaken. There are probably some around you are still very deeply connected to your past. It's their last point of reference, because as you were growing and maturing, they remained stuck. Those are the character types that you must stay away from when you have determined to build anything in life. Find a center of people who see what you're working towards and won't let you quit even when you give them the best excuses why you should.

I can vividly recall calling my mentor and explaining to him the reasons why I should discontinue building in a particular area. My argument was strong. My points were valid. But they just didn't carry enough weight because much of it was emotionally based. Much of the want that we must quit isn't because it can't work. It's because of the pressure of waiting while it does.

That's how we are sometimes when we experience challenges when building towards greatness. We know the impact that it will have on our personal worlds, but at that moment it seems like we don't have enough to make it to the end. Having the right people around you will take some of the exasperation away, and they'll be able to provide relief during some of your most distracted moments.

ALLOWING DESTINY TO WIN

One of the things that I love is how destiny pulls us so far up the road that turning around isn't an option anymore. We're already beyond the halfway point and the distance to get to the end is the same distance to get back to the beginning. At this point, it would really cost more to turn around then it would to keep going. This must be how you now view your building project whatever it may be. The idea of turning around is no longer an option. You're looking at it, and it seems like it's costing you so much, but what you must realize is that if you stop now it will cost you so much more.

I want you to accept something. Whether you realize it or not something in you needs to accomplish this. You're hearing a cry from a stronger voice now. It's your own. For once in your life you need to know that you're not a failure and that giving up isn't an option for you. Yes! You've already accomplished a lot and probably more than anyone in your family. You're successful, but it's not enough. Don't allow your choice a chance. Let me explain what I mean by this. Many of us have used choice as a weapon against finishing. Just because we can, we do. This must change. You need to finish this! No Excuses. Just finish.

Just think for a moment about the individual that decides to build a home. If you've built one, you already know where I'm going. Do you know how many things come up adversely when you are doing so? You might have soil problems, permit issues, material shortages, issues with contractors etc., but most of the time you don't just give up on the project. You keep building. It might take you a little longer, but you don't stop.

In this same example, it's sometimes sad to ride pass lots where a house had started to be built, but for some reason couldn't continue. I don't want this to be the way your plan turns out. In this chapter, I'll share with you more thoughts and keys to overcoming some of the challenges and distractions you might encounter as you build something great.

Aaron J. Mobley, Jr.

KEEP IT MOVING!
OPPOSITION TO YOUR MOVEMENT IS A STRATEGY AGAINST YOUR GROWTH

You're finally picking up speed and gaining momentum. The sigh of relief you let out when you're finally able to see the fruit of your labor is exhilarating. There's nothing like it. You're now able to proudly announce to those that doubted you that "I did it". For all the tears and sweat you know have something that you can put your hands on and display as a product of your heart.

I wish that I could write and tell you that at this point nothing would ever come again to stop you, but as you know, I can't. For every level of momentum, you experience there's a greater level of opposition that fights to either keep you at that level or push you back to your starting point. I want to ask you a question. At what point are you willing to stop building? When is enough success enough for you?

There are some individuals who's ultimate goal is to purchase a home while there are others who just won't stop there. They want to own the entire neighborhood. Only you have the power to choose what your ultimate level of success is, and you've got to allow other to choose as well. Sometimes we look at someone else's passion and think how low the pursuit is or how much more they can be doing. But the truth is, that what makes them fulfilled might be something that has nothing to do with what brings happiness to you. Respecting another individual's right to pursue their dreams and goals is the character of honor that will always bring the spotlight on yours.

So, whatever your goal is, don't allow anything to stop your momentum towards it. Here's two things that you must understand about momentum:

Movement produces the energy to grow. Whenever you start to gain momentum you automatically produce an energy to grow. You are coming up with new ideas, new ways to better what you've done and you're probably even scouting out new places to implement your idea in.

Growth is a scary idea to those who despise your success and whatever they must do to stop it they will. I know we don't want to ever have to imagine that someone might work against me it's the reality of human existence. Whether it's in business, social arenas or everyday life, there will always be those who for someone reason don't want to see you succeed and in order to stop you from succeeding they have to stop you from moving. I want you to think about your life and the things that have come to oppose you. Did it stop you from moving? Did everything stop when it happened? If so, it wasn't just an attack against you or your plan, it was an attack against your momentum. Momentum builds force and in the right hands it can throw a powerful punch.

Opposition to movement is a strategy against growth. Anything or anyone that opposes your movement opposes your growth. What this simply means is that any time a person attempts to restrict or limit your travel towards destiny they are clearly attacking your growth. Growth in any area of life needs your movement. You need to get out and seek. You must go to places where your gift will be exposed. You have to change and advance your companions. All these things take movement.

Letting others convince you to stay with them in their passivity cannot be your mindset any longer. You've got to break free. This might mean moving from city to city, changing professions, social activities or more, but start by identifying people and situations that have limited your movement. These will be the main reasons that you are not growing and building.

So, after all of that, what's stopped you? Who have you allowed to enter your life (or resurface) and cause you to put on pause what

2

was on fast forward? It amazes me how we can allow circumstances to pull us all the way back when we had gone so far. Believe me. I know exactly how this can happen and how it's not so easily conquered as some would have us believe, but we've got to fight against it. We have to develop habits and structures in our lives that build a discipline within us that if it ever comes back, we'll not only recognize it but avoid it at all costs. Just let it go. Keep your eyes on the finished product. The process might be a little cumbersome at times, but always remember what you're working for. You'll get there.

KEEP YOUR PERSPECTIVE DURING UNFORESEEN CHALLENGES

Just because you're not experiencing a great thrust of achievement now does not mean that somehow you have missed the mark. We are sometimes so quick to blame ourselves for events that are honestly just in the process. I think at some point in all of our lives we have looked at these great pauses and said, "I wonder if I'm to blame" or "If I really had it like everyone said it would be moving a little easier. Maybe this is not for me". This is the wrong way to think when you experience challenge. You do have what it takes. If it's a goal in your heart, it's just not supposed to stay there. You're supposed to go after it and be willing to do what you can to achieve it.

Some things were just meant to be the way they were until you arrived to a certain point in life. It was yours. But certain events had to transpire to bring it pass. There are moments that I can't explain why this while I personally experience life, but I've found it to be true. Something powerful is going to happen. The only thing that you must do is stay in the game long enough to see it.

EVERY SEASON PRESENTS AN OPPORTUNITY TO PROMOTE PURPOSE. USE IT TO "YOUR" ADVANTAGE. MAKE EVERYTHING PURPOSEFUL

Some of the greatest tools that will make your building strong are the ugliest of situations, the most difficult of circumstances and the things that made you cry the hardest. Use it all. Don't allow any materials to be wasted. If you went through it for any reason, it was meant to strengthen an area that you probably don't realize exist. It's really to move on as if certain situations didn't happen, but there is nothing like being empowered through an experience that really should have killed you and your dreams. Just think about it. You are stronger today as a visionary because of many of the lessons that you learned during those pressured seasons. Your resilience is outstanding, and you have learned the value of pressing beyond them and continuing to look towards the finish. Use it all.

One of the distinctive characteristics in true life builders is that they can take an unexpected or under-resourced situation and make it look intentional. They have a calmness about themselves that doesn't allow them to overact during emergencies. They find a way to navigate through that situation and make it useful. So, it's happened huh? Ok. What now? How can you use what may look like a disaster (and feel like a disaster to you) useful? How can you recycle the garbage of some of life's experiences? Guess what. Most of it isn't garbage at all. It's just the building blocks that you need to reinforce this massive vision that will literally change the world. Your perception of life's experiences will prove to be the energy needed to move beyond them effectively while accomplishing steps towards your dreams every day.

YOU'VE NOT WASTED ANY TIME!

What discourages us sometimes is the idea that we've wasted time. Even the thought that we've spent years going after something that might not happen. That's enough to make anyone discouraged. However, I'm not sure if I have the words necessary to explain to you how intentional the process of your life has been. We don't sometimes see that far ahead. Every now and again, we get the pleasure of seeing glimpses and peeks into the future, but not as often as we would like. Even when we do, what's often missing in the view are the people that will stop supporting us, the resources that will stop flowing, the loss of ambition and the many other distractions that will come in the middle. But even in perspective to all these things, as long as you are connected to purpose you are not wasting anything. Through every season, learn to use everything and everyone in it to get you to the end.

Believe me when I tell you that everything that you have experienced will be well worth it if you stick with it. You'll see.

Here's a few things I want you to remember as we move forward:

Serve your time of waiting well by using it to prepare for sudden opportunity: You don't want opportunity to show up while you're still getting dressed. Isn't that one of the most irritating things to have happened to you? You go to pick someone up, and you've previously told them what time you would be arriving, and you get there, and they are nowhere near ready. That's just how we are sometimes when opportunity comes. We've wasted all our waiting time doing what...WAITING that we literally forgot to keep getting ready.

It doesn't matter if you've been going over that business plan for the last five years, and no one wants to invest in it. Keep making it ready. Every year should have resulted in more relevant information being added to it that brings it current. Don't miss a good thing because you forgot to get prepared.

Don't fall asleep while waiting, because you assume it's not coming: In the same scenario, let's switch positions. So, you're the person that's waiting, and they are just not showing up. In most cases, we just get undressed, because we assume that they're not going to get there, or our attitudes are so terrible that they wouldn't want us to be around if they did show up.

This is how we are when it comes to our dreams and visions. It doesn't take a lot for some people to fall asleep on their dreams and jump on the nearest train elsewhere. However, as long as you're still connected to it and are sourcing it with your attention it's going to show up. Just keep working on it while you wait. Anything worth waiting for is also worth working for.

Re-train yourself to EXPECTSUCCESS AGAIN: The truth is that some of us are gun shy. We've tried some of everything and it seems like nothing has worked. While there are others who once were successful, but it seems like they just can't get to that level of success again, so they stop expecting it.

Reset your mind to expect success not only in the level you saw it in previously but also greater than that. The way you think has a large role in how your building towards greatness plays out.

Ready or not. Here it comes: If opportunity showed up right now would you be ready? Not just ready in the sense of you being tired of waiting, but I'm talking about ready to work it. Opportunity doesn't just come to give you a check. Opportunity comes as a tool to advance your purpose and your passion. Are you ready?

Much of our present frustration might not be because opportunity didn't arrive. It's likely because we had nothing prepared when it did.

STAYING CONNECTED
RESISTING THE URGE TO LOWER YOUR EXPECTATIONS

There's something somewhere that is already succeeding without you. Let me explain this clearly. It's already in its best state just waiting on you to show up and make the connection. Sometimes we think that we're moving towards the goal in order for us to make things better, but what if the thing you're working for has the potential of making everything you know better just because you connected with it. It's like the oil field that has yet to be tapped. No one knows that it's there. The oil hasn't been discovered and is filled with the potential not only to be fuel to others, but also wealth to some.

Let's fill in a gap that I think many people miss when pursuing a vision, dream, or goal. As long as you live, there will always be someone that will have the ability to advance you. Yes, you are doing your own work and overcoming your own challenges, but there will always be someone or something that will make the connection from goal to goal. Maintaining an attitude that you don't need anyone or help with anything will always keep you stuck.

No one has the power to make you, but what they may have is resources to help you. What they might have are connections that get you in the door of opportunity or they just may be able to bring exposure to the product that you already have, but that no one knows about. I want you to begin to open your mind to making quality connections.

Quality connections are partnerships on various levels that advance what you have to offer to a particular situation. They aren't the ones that keep you stuck at a certain level or what we would call the "glass ceiling". They are literally connections that see what you are bringing to the table as valuable and worth promoting. How many individuals in your life can you call a "Quality Connection"?

VISIONS AND VEHICLES

I want you to begin to think of your project or plan as a vehicle of transportation. Start asking yourself some questions. Where is it taking me? How often do I fuel it? And what am I putting in my tank? It will amaze you how stuck your life can be when you are not refueling or how sluggish it can be when you are refueling with the wrong things. Think about it.

The work that you are currently undertaking is only work to get you somewhere. It's the vehicle that's chosen to bring you into an area that I like to call your "Place of Response. Your place of response is an area of life that automatically comes alive when you show up.

Many of you reading this are known in your circle as the life of the party. You've probably said things like this, "The party doesn't start until I get there". Your personality fills a room and even without you saying a word thing begin to change. Excitement exudes you in every way. This is how your "Place of Response" reacts to you. Everything in it and everyone connected to it recognizes who you are. It's kind of like it knew to expect you and continued to mature and develop until you did.

So, you're probably asking what a "Place of Response"? A place of response can be a city, profession, person, opportunity, passion, hobby, etc.

What's important is that you don't get tired of the THING that's going to get you there. Yeah, you should have known I was going there. We often get tired of working the plan, developing the vehicle that will ultimately get us to this place of success. Stay connected with it!

As messed up or unpresentable as your vehicle is sometimes if it can still get you to your destinations it's still worth having until you can purchase something else. Why don't we see our visions like that? No, it's not as elaborate as others or as polished as the persons next door, but it's still workable. You still have time to get it polished. The more you travel with it, the more it grows in stability and endurance. Your vision is taking you somewhere great!

Refuse to move away from the place where you know success is going to show up.

Believe me when I tell you that I know how people will encourage you to leave when it doesn't happen quickly enough for you. Sometimes it's out of concern, but sometimes it's also because they've never worked for anything for a long length of time too. They can't see beyond their personal levels of experience.

Learn how to value the perspective and opinions of others, but not allow them to cause you to forfeit what is REAL to you. Some of the things that you are working on are honestly another person's fairytale life. They wished that they have the strength to overcome that you have. They long to have the passion that you have in certain areas. When they don't manage their personal regrets well, it will all come down on you in the worst ways. It's up to you to always understand where someone is coming from and not allow their experiences to dampen what you see as destiny. Thanks, but no thanks.

Make the choice to stay connected to the "Thing". Whatever it is and whatever is purpose for you. One day sooner than later it's going to carry you to a place where you might not need it anymore.

Okay, here's a bonus thought: Don't always assume that the vision you're currently working towards is always going to be the thing that you'll use to succeed. Some things are merely achievements towards a greater goal. That's why you can't get stuck. So, you're having to get a degree in an area that doesn't interest you in an area that does. Be willing to lay solid foundations of growth that will foster future generations of success. Learn how to overcome distractions and obstacles because you just might need the same tools to get over something on another level in a different day.

Lowered Expectations

One of the killers to your destiny will always be "Lowered Expectations". The danger in lowered expectations is that you sometimes only prepare for what you expect to arrive. Therefore, limiting yourself on how much of the promise you can keep. This is like you are going to the store and you've already prepared in your mind the amount of money you'll need. You only take with you a certain amount because that's as much as you're going to spend. You've convinced yourself. While for budgeting purposes this might work great, but where it relates to enjoying your place of response it's a bad idea.

Consequently, you get to the store and remember that you left half of the items off your list, and you don't have enough money to buy those items. You now must go back home and get the rest of your money or leave the items that you really need. You've also now wasted the time you needed to prepare, but most of all enjoy. Use the time you now have while building to expand your ability to receive. Make room in your mind for the day where you'll have more than enough resources to build what you want in the manner that you wish. Don't lower your expectations.

Lowering expectations also has to do with how we view the success of others. We look at what they have and automatically assume that it's as easy as it appears. For the bonafide builder, they are working tirelessly behind the scenes to make strides just like you are. On the other hand, some people only have what looks like success, but underneath it is nothing that you would want. They're extremely in debt and can't find a way to get out. Let's make it clear. Life happens to us all, but the thought is not to lower your expectations based on an idea you see in someone else's life until you know the story of how they got to where they are. Because maybe they aren't any farther along than you are.

Be careful not to lower your expectations in the assumption that if I make it smaller that it will come sooner.

One of the methods we use to attempt to make success come faster is that we make it smaller. We cut off so much of the building that it's no longer a house anymore, it's a driveway with a garage that we sleep in. Why? Because we just wanted to be done. Guess what? That's still not an accomplishment. You simply erased the plan and started another one. Choose to accomplish things as you set out to. If it was a certain job, house, dream, or vision, achieve it as you first imagined. You'll have to work at it, but don't cut it up just because you're getting tired of waiting.

Find ways that you can benefit from the plan while you are building. What are some ways that you can use the process to provide for you as you are continuing to develop greatness in your life? Every stage of the process has the possibility of providing a resource for you. At one stage, you might work a second job to get you through school or at another stage you might sell those handmade clothes you've designed since you were a child as you pursue a fashion career. You can use wherever you are as a tool to make your life great. Whatever you do, don't make it smaller. If you choose to do anything, make it larger.

Aaron J. Mobley, Jr.

COMMITTING TO THE PROCESS

H aving a great idea, but not having the commitment needed to see it happen is a waste. You do know that the world is filled with individuals who are full of great ideas, right? You can turn on the television right now, read the newspaper or simply listen to the conversations around you and find individuals who are consumed with awesome ideas or products. Sadly, many of those ideas will be carried out by someone else. Yes, there will be many individuals who will make money and success off what you are keeping locked in your head if you don't do something about it.

I think we sometimes assume that our ideas are simply our own. We believe that we can sit on them for years untapped, and no one will ever think of it. Some of you who are reading this, know firsthand the danger in having this type of attitude. I don't care how much you guard your secret or put it down on a piece of paper underneath your mattress it's bound to get out. Maybe not with all the personal embellishments, but certainly in foundation.

How many of you have ever had a really good idea? You were convinced that it had the potential of making you highly successful. There wasn't anything on the market close to what you had just thought of, but the only thing that stopped you was that at that point in your life you didn't have the focus needed to work towards it.

You put it down in your journal and may have even shared it with a few people, but nothing ever came of it. You couldn't give it the attention that it needed. I don't even have to finish this thought, but I will. You then turn on the television or walk into the store and there it is. The idea that you've had for the longest is being sold and profited by someone else. The regret that comes is the worst. You look at your life and say, "If only I had done something with this idea". For some of us, this has happened repeatedly. You cannot afford to wait. Your dreams are calling you. Answer them before someone else does.

I'm sure someone is asking this question. How does this happen? Wasn't this a God-given idea that belonged to me and if it is, why did someone else think of the same thing? Let's think of it this way. An idea is simply a strain of thoughts that require fulfillment. Someone must make it happen. If one person won't it travels to another until it is. Why? Because the earth needs it. Do you honestly think that if the car hadn't pursued it that we would still be driving in wagons pulled by horses? That's absurd. Whenever you refuse to move on a divinely inspired thought, you literally push it off on someone else who just might be diligent enough to do something with it.

What's interesting about this line of thought is that some of you were the first in line. This means that you were selected as the first person to ever have it. How it proceeds down the line is totally up to you. The truth is that some individuals are chosen to carry some ideas, because of the process that they've undergone internally to develop it. Greatness is never carried on the back of the weak of heart. It's managed by those who have personally endured the roughest of times and the most difficult of circumstances.

So, what have you been given as a first? And just maybe it's already on the market. What have you been given that you can further build to make it better or greater than the thing that's come before it? You can be the next creator of a more advanced design. Don't stop because you think your idea or plan is lost. There's a sharper edge that you might be given to place on an idea that's lost its effect.

I want to encourage you to be the individual that is always responsible for the gifts that you have been given. Can you be trusted to produce something great? Will you be accountable to it? Will you do whatever you have to to make it happen? How this idea plays out will be totally up to you.

GIVE IT SOME TIME. IT'S GROWING.

I want you to start thinking of every year that has passed as necessary to develop what was not matured in the previous season. In some instances, it needed to take this long. Longer processes produce stronger, longer-lasting products. Every process that you undergo in building your dream is ultimately pushing you towards a greater place. COMPLETE THE PICTURE.

Whether you realize it or not, every day that goes by adds something on to your vision. Sometimes we are so discouraged because we feel that we've done everything we can. Our simple tasks have already been done, and we can't think of anything that we can do to make it happen faster. We don't have the money to pay for it or the people to help us build it. So, we sit and wonder whether it will truly ever happen for it.

The encouragement is that the picture is being completed with and without your help. Oh yes, this is going to take your full effort. But even the organization behind the scenes in your life is major. There are people, situations, and opportunities that are being set-up on your behalf that you are clueless about. If the dream that you have is authentic to the design of God for your life, it's going to happen. Honor every moment, because in doing this you value the times that God has been authorized to bring you something needed to complete the picture of your purpose.

TAKE THE TIME TO LISTEN

What are you listening to? Each moment in your life reveals valuable truths. These are lessons that help you move forward. Listen, you've got to get going. These revelations aren't only limited to your life as an individual, but everything that is connected to it. Remember that it's not only about you. It's about your family, friends, community, and well beyond that. You are destined to impact the world in ways that you can't even imagine, but you must take the time to listen. Begin to evaluate every area of your life accurately. Hear what it's saying presently and the instructions it gives to move beyond past failure.

What is today saying about your future? Don't evaluate your life and present circumstances by feeling bad. Make the choice to listen in joy because it provides what you need to push you to your next. Don't just keep sitting there. The moment where you are is trying to give you something. Say yes and thank you.

VISION EMPOWERS THE PROCESS

A simple way to think about vision is your ability to know what is real in a future day.... but RIGHT NOW! It's not just some spooky occurrence that throws you in a deep trance as some would have you believe. In a very practical sense, it is your practical ability to realize an idea that you already know is going to happen.

Many of our dreams and visions are never realized because in our hearts we never had vision. What we had was a great idea or a creative thought, but vision wasn't anywhere around. Vision is forceful. It's the energy that assists you during some of your darkest days. Have you ever wondered how people can move thousands of miles away without any money, without a place to live only to go after something that they dreamed as a child? It's not just a pipe dream in most cases. It's vision. Vision will help you to suffer for what you really believe is your reality.

It's almost impossible to ever really have a vision and then forget about it. Why? Because in your heart you know it as a reality. It's kind of like traveling back from a future date. There is no human being that can convince you that certain events will not happen because you've already seen them. You know that it exists. Here's a word of caution. What's real to you might not be real to anyone else but you. You're going to have to be strong enough to look crazy while it's manifested. What you'll discover is that what people have called your crazy for doing will be the training ground for how they pursue their dreams in the future. Most people only need someone in their life that they can pattern themselves after and they'll find themselves doing the same radical things.

Take the time to begin to jot down things in your life that are good thoughts and then those that are visions. Good thoughts are those things that you use as "resource" agents. It's the in-between work. The in-between work can be defined as the things that you use to bring provision to your life as you build towards vision. Don't ever be ashamed of your in-between work. It gives you the substance needed to experience full vision when it comes.

Having vision is also not just the reality of future events. It's the literal push behind your process. Understanding what vision to you is early will help you to not only recognize it when it starts to happen, but it'll also give you the added push needed step-by-step.

VISION IS A PLAN, A SET OF GOALS AND INITIATIVES THAT ARE PLACED IN MOTION ACCORDING TO REVELATION!

Vision is also a set of goals that are linked by revelation. What's the complete picture? How have you seen it unfold? What are the steps that you see necessary to see it come to pass?

Whatever the steps are, one of the main ingredients that you'll need is most certainly Faith. You've got to have faith in what you have seen and where it has come from. You can't see your dream or vision as just something that came out of nowhere. It must be something that you know is from God. Not too many people ever arrive at that level of faith, because many of our plans are just sketches. They are the products of random thoughts that we feel can work. This level of faith cannot be like that. It's not what you feel can work. It's what you know is going to work with the right amount of effort, sacrifice, and support. Have faith.

Here are a couple of points that I hope will help you along your journey of faith towards the incredible vision you have:

Faith causes you to see what's there, but not there yet: Faith is designed to make you aware of those things that are already existing beyond your human senses. Those things are permanently fixed in your future and only realized naturally as you believe that they are.

Understand the greatness of what you are seeing: Learn to prepare for a large outcome based on a SMALLS signs. Understand the momentum that sometimes follow insignificant starts. Don't prepare for vision compared to the size of the start, but according to the size of the finish. Often, we only prepare for what we see. The key is to see your vision in fullness. It will help you to prepare for all of it and just not small portions.

Lastly, committing to the process is more than just saying that you have vision or that you have faith. It's your conscious agreement to every step and moment that you're ordained to walk through. It's going backwards and forwards at the same time. You know where you're going and every day going through the motions to get back there. Take a deep breath and then GET BACK TO VISION! You've already seen it. Now go get what's yours. You can do it. I believe in you!

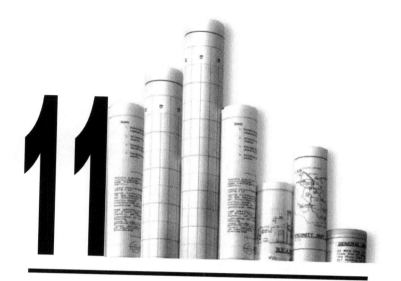

DEVELOPING STORM STRATEGIES

O ne day something is going to come to attempt to disrupt your flow of greatness. It'll be during a time when you most likely see the most productivity you have experienced since you decided to go after your dreams. I'm not saying this to dampen the excitement you are feeling, but to show you that anything can be overcome with a solid strategy. However, finding a strategy that works for you takes some work. Unfortunately, sometimes you don't know what works until you try it. Only then you'll be able to scrap what doesn't and keep what does. Considering this, I don't want you to be afraid to walk various methods out. Truthfully, some things distract others while those same things have no effect on the rest. Each journey of greatness is particular to the person designed to walk that path out. I'm assuming that by this point in your life, you probably know what your trigger points are.

Trigger points are a different level of distraction. They are more emotional in nature because they are normally attached to memories and areas within yourself and your past. Trigger points are like the street that you avoid passing because of the trauma you experienced in a house on that block, hearing the name of a person that has offended you, a particular color that reminds you of a bad experience or the smell of cologne that connects you back to an old relationship. It's important to know these areas because if you are ever careless you could walk on a minefield that might have the potential of destroying your goals.

Especially, if you are not prepared to tiptoe through it.

One of the methods that I have learned through the years to avoid distractions and unhealthy trigger points is to manage my communication. Thankfully, most of us have a strong circle of confidants that we can share, receive advice, and listen to. With those individuals, you don't have to in most cases guard your heart around. You can open your ears freely because you know that what's coming in them will help and not hurt. Unfortunately, confidants aren't the only people in our world. Some individuals aren't as concerned about your progress as you are. It's those connections that you must evaluate at what level they have access to you as you're building towards greatness.

Managing communication takes diligence. You can't be thirsty for applause, recognition, or praise. What you're training yourself to do is to focus on what builds and stay away from those conversations that don't. For most of us, we already feel like we're a little late in pursuing our dreams. We're working overtime to make sure that our children or families have the opportunities that we've always wanted for them. So, the last thing that we have time to accommodate is negativity from conversations, situations, or people that we let it. This is where managing communication becomes priority.

Here's a few questions that I hope will help you in managing communication more wisely:

What role does this person have in my life? Is this a short-term or long-term connection?

Knowing what a person's role and commitment in your life will assist you in recognizing their level of access. If you acknowledge that someone will be in your life for a short period of time, it might be wise to allow them into some of the most intimate places of your heart, dreams, or vision. Doing this might cause harm and delays to your momentum when they depart. Choose to invest in those that you view as long term partners.

What effect will this conversation have on my movement?

Some conversations will literally stop you from moving. It's not that you aren't aware of this, but for some reason you still entertain them. If someone has a pattern of saying negative or disruptive things to you or are constantly bringing up your trigger points, stay away. Train yourself to be more attentive to productive levels of communication. You'll begin developing at a more rapid pace if you refuse to open the door for discouragement from individuals who may not support your vision anyway.

How have I communicated my expectations to others?

Everyone in your intimate circle and world should know what you expect regarding what they say to you during your building process. You don't need to hear every rumor, point of gossip or discouraging comment about your plan. Many individuals are delayed in what they know can work but stop midstream because of how others may feel about it. You can't become delayed because of hearing something if you don't hear it. Close your ears and make sure that everyone in your world knows what you expect. Also, if you find that they won't respect your request and continue to share discouraging comments, then it might possibly be because of their personal feeling about what you are doing. That would be someone that you shouldn't have onboard as well. Get to the bottom of it and move forward.

Why is it important to me?

Our willingness to open damaging doors of communication can often times be a sign that we ourselves are not confident in what we're doing. Therefore, there is constantly a need to be validated by something on the outside. So, if they say it's no good, we stop or if they say they like it we continue.

WHY NOW AND WHY THIS?

The more your build your life and family the more attempts will come in various forms to make you either slow down or stop entirely. You don't have to do anything to make it happen it's inevitable. The only question that must be asked within yourself is why.

Why is this distraction coming now? What opportunity lies ahead that it's attempting to push me away from? Yes, it's easy to sit and take it as a personal attack, but what I've discovered is that many scenarios have very little to do with you as an individual and more to do with the thing that you are creating. What I want you to begin developing in your mind is that what your hands are currently connected to is designed to give you power and control. This is one of the greatest lessons that I have been taught and press towards every day of my life. It is the understanding that I am supposed to have power in every sphere of my life. It is my divine right to be in authority financially, emotionally, spiritually, relationally and every other area that I might be attached to. It is not being in control that many times opens the door for debilitating distractions.

Debilitating distractions are those storms that seem to come out of nowhere. You're not prepared for them and most of all, you don't have a plan on how to ride them out. They literally immobilize you in fear because you cannot control them. It's kind of like experiencing a great storm that has caused significant damage, and there's no insurance to help you rebuild. You are not in control. I'm sure that without a second guess, you can think of several times presently or in the past where you have not been in control of a situation. How did it make you feel? Were you fearful and why?

As we move towards a greater level of productivity, one of the things that we must establish in our lives is an expectation of distractions. You know that what you're building is great and that in many cases it is life impacting to those that experience it. So, it's expected that opposition is going to come. You've got to set up some principles against distraction NOW. It can't wait.

I want to go through a few scenarios for why storms come right in the middle of your greatest level of growth.

Let's go through a few scenarios for why storms come while building great:

1. REPOSITIONING AND REPLANTING

Honestly, we don't know everything, and sometimes we plant our visions in the wrong places with the best of intentions. Of course, at the time it seems right, but as we attempt to develop them there something seems not to be working. There will be occasions where you will either need to be **Repositioned** or **Replanted**. Often, our effectiveness in the assignment we are given is solely dependent on the **PLACE** where we are attempting to do it in.

REMEMBER EVERY ASSIGNMENT IS CONNECTED TO A PLACE OF RESPONSE. What causes the response of the assignment on your life is the need for it **IN THE PLACE** where it's chosen to thrive. It's extremely hard to be successful in a disobedient place. We often go in opposite directions to our heart, because we have trained that it's emotionally led, but sometimes it's just a clear understanding of where you should go and what you should be doing.

Choosing to go left when you are supposed to go right will always result in a storm developing. It's the nature of our purpose to attract what it needs to to get us back on the correct track. You just might be drawing something to yourself that you don't necessarily like. Evaluate today whether you're headed in the right direction. Repositioning and replanting yourself might be the calm in the storm you need to continue building more effectively.

2. YOU'RE BEING REMOVED YOU FROM SOMETHING:

There are simply some things and people that you can't be connected to ANYMORE! I believe that much of our success is halted because of our refusal to listen to what we hear inside. Your building is not meant to house everyone. Especially, those who will not value the work that you put towards it to get it where it is. Look in your world today and notice those who are actually pushing you forward. In the world of the builder, the numbers are sometimes very few, but the crowds are so large. Not everyone in your audience is cheering you own. Learn to detach easily from those who are not true supporters. Choosing to carry them along might end up being very deadly to your dream and vision. Watch for opportunities to disconnect from unproductive places smoothly. Don't prolong the process through some emotional type of tug of war. Take the first door, because it's the additional doors that must be opened that usually cause the most damage.

- **Be aware of silent followers:** Silent followers are unproductive attachments that are not supporting you publically, but for some reason won't disconnect. When individuals are truly in your corner, they don't mind speaking up for you or your vision.

- **Be aware of the watchers:** Watchers are those individuals who are just looking for some area of to find fault in. They stay close not to reinforce you in vision, but to point out areas of weakness to those who might be supporting you. It doesn't matter how elaborate your vision is they will always find some area to find an issue with.

3. IT'S AN ATTEMPT TO TAKE AWAY OR TO KEEP YOU AWAY FROM SOMETHING: Be aware of the MIND GAMES:

Much of what causes us to want to quit is not physical occurrences. Most of the reasons come from the weariness that we experience in our minds. The constant battle to balance what we feel and what we know with who's supporting and who's not is sometimes too much for us to handle.

Mental exertion will cause your efforts to completely stop. You'll know what the goal is and how it's attainable but lack the willpower to continue. You're now convinced that what you saw wasn't real at all. It's just a game. Don't be fooled.

You can also be tricked into denying who we are because of what you feel has happened to you. Surely, if I were some great wonder all of these storms would not have showed up on my doorsteps, right? WRONG. It is absolutely because you are that they have. The integrity of what you are building must be qualified. Are you willing to go through the inspection process?

When you are building a home or purchasing one, it is a standard practice to have it inspected. The inspector looks for things that aren't seen with the naked eye. They look for areas that might have been overlooked or built poorly. Should they find an area that needs attention, the buyer or builder has an opportunity to correct the issue before moving forward. We often get frustrated during storms, because we know the work that we might possibly have to do to get it moving forward. This is not the heart of a true builder. Whatever you build you want it to be right. Choose to change your perspective from thinking that it's all about you. It's about what you've been chosen to build that matters.

Your effectiveness in building is solely dependent on the principal thought you have concerning yourself and your role in the building process. Therefore, one of the target assignments against you might be to damage the THOUGHT that you have concerning yourself. If your expectation can be lowered, it will literally stunt the height of your building project. Think well of yourself.

Aaron J. Mobley, Jr.

MASTERING THE SMALL PLACES

The reality in life is that at some point you'll want to have more. It's not that you're being materialistic or superficial.

You've just grown up. Sometimes when we were younger, we didn't see the need for growth in certain areas. We lived a carefree life and didn't concern ourselves with much about future planning and strategy. To us, we were just living for the current day on the calendar. But as time would have it, we all grew up and discovered that we did need more to ensure a stable future for ourselves and families.

When things start growing or expanding it requires a little more attention and resources than it did before. It's kind of like the kid whose shoe size grows every month. It's always time for another pair. Believe it or not, that's just how our life is when we submit to the growing process. We find out things that we honestly enjoy, and then we come to the startling revelation that there were some things that we were doing that we absolutely hated.

We all want more, whether we're willing to admit it, there is some part of our life that is requiring something that we can't currently provide. The cost of life itself demands that in some way or another we are growing in every area but supplying every area doesn't sometimes seem that easy.

I wanted to begin the task of concluding this book by sharing personal thoughts on how God uses small or seemingly insignificant assignments to prepare and prove us. Every period of your life will be proving ground for the period that is next. Refusing to get prepared or developed in that season only works against you. This is one of the top reasons why some of us are not moving forward. We won't take time seriously by using it as a lesson. For some people, time is simply a game. It's something that is toyed with until there is nothing left. If you are to build towards greatness, this cannot be the pattern that you choose. You must value time and use it as an opportunity to advance. This means that every day you live is an open door to walking closer to dream fulfillment and destiny.

What's in your hands? I want you to begin looking at what your hands are currently holding or attached to. What are you actively working on now as an assignment or task? An assignment or task in relation to this chapter is simply a duty that hopefully will lead you to a greater understanding of destiny. It's the thing that is building your work ethics and working out of you those characteristics that might mess up your plan in the future. This is important because many of us are so destiny bound that we forget our responsibility to work a duty.

Your faithfulness in the small places is what promotes a greater understanding of what you've been sincerely called to build. Always be cautious of individuals who refuse to do something while they are working on something. It's the work in the middle that really gets you ready not sitting while twiddling your thumbs. What's that thing that you despise doing, but it's helping to prepare you for a greater goal? Pay attention to your answers. They mean more to your process than you know.

If we're not careful, we will begin to qualify assignments based on the size and measurement of it. The larger ones get the most of our attention while the smaller tasks get little or none. With this mindset, it is almost impossible to ever see the potential of the seeds that you are sowing in your life, family, business, or others.

THE POWER OF A SEED

It's hard to fully release a seed into the ground when you are not confident of its connection to a greater outcome. For example, the farmer who has taken care of his resources to buy a field with the intent to plant must know confidently that if he plants correctly and does the work needed that it will bring a return. It must leave his hands in confidence. Your dream can sense the confidence that you sow into or the lack thereof. I know that this might sound weird, but opportunities are attracted to individuals who are confident. Who wants to hire a potential employee who isn't confident that they'll be able to do the job? What's your confidence level right now? If the right opportunity showed up would you rush into it or would you be afraid that you couldn't do the job?

Everything that you are currently a part of must be thought of as being connected to a much larger purpose. Not thinking this way will result in you being constantly irritated and frustrated. Have you ever wondered why to some it is difficult to lend a helping hand, support another individual or encourage anyone else? Let me share with you one reason why. They can't see it as being a seed used to make them successful in a future point of time. We sometimes live such disconnected lives that it's hard for us to ever see the dollar that we give to the homeless person on the corner as being connected to the million that someone invests in our business in future years. I think if we thought of it in that way, we would see more generosity not only in our lives but in the world itself. We are all connected. Everything is connected.

The power of seeing something great come from a small task is found in your willingness to embrace it. Not condescendingly but embrace it just as if it were the greatest opportunity you had ever been given. Have you ever considered that your life is just the active ingredient someone needs? Your partnership with a duty might just push someone else's dream forward while giving you the necessary preparation to build one day your own. What are you learning where you are now? Someone reading this might say, "Well, I'm just the secretary". But you're not just the secretary. You have the opportunity to learn, and also observe. Whatever you are doing has to be more to you than just the title that is attached to it. Repeat this: "I am more than what I'm doing".

Here's a few points to help you Master the Small Places:

Choose to surround yourself with those honor your small place just as much as you do while encouraging you to look forward to greater.

There's nothing more discouraging then to become excited over an opportunity and then get around your friends and they mock you because of it. Choose to surround yourself with individuals who see what you're doing as a valuable and necessary steppingstone.

Greatness has little to do with where you are and more to do with how you honor where you are.

We automatically honor things and people that we place value on. Become intentional about being grateful for the small doors that seem insignificant to others. Honor will always bring you before great opportunities.

Recognize the potential of small places.

Don't be so quick to dismiss what you view as a small assignment as having no benefit. Learn to recognize the potential in that one thing to become greater. Think of the balloon. It's small in nature but has expanding quality. Many opportunities will come your way. Recognize the ones that have the potential to grow beyond what they look like.

Your potential greatness is confirmed through how you handle opposition when things are still small.

True greatness is tested in small places. Your ability to persevere through opposition in the small places of your life will be the pattern you set for the challenges that come in great doors. How are you currently handling difficulties? Don't welcome greater ones if you haven't first mastered the small ones that have shown up.

Increase where you are.

There is no need to stop the growing process of your dreams until you get there. Let the vision expand within you by planning it out and by continuing to add on to it until it bursts through the seams of your life. Grow where you are. Doors open best when you become too big where you are. No limits! No borders! Keep growing.

Hopefully, these points will help you appreciate the growing process. Sometimes we don't jump into the more exposed places of greatness before we can value every road that will get us there. Every journey has the potential to become great when you determine to master and value them.

Aaron J. Mobley, Jr.

MAKING IT REALITY

All of us have something that we can use to form and build. It's called our imagination. For most of us, when we were children we would sit and imagine worlds and situations that didn't even exist around us. Some of you even had imaginary friends who would assist you in your mischief or who would sit politely as you poured them fake tea.

I think we lost the power of imagination as we grew up and started to experience real life circumstances. We lost the ability to see ourselves in a world that might just look better that what we see today. I wonder what would happen if you were to sit right now and imagine what your world would look like when your dream is fulfilled.

I like to call this "Creative Imagination". It's not just the act of making up things or living in a fantasy world. It's putting the pieces together internally before anyone ever sees them in real life. It's expanding how you view your life, dreams, and visions. How much larger can you make it?

Experiencing Wipe Out

One of the obstacles to many of us creatively imagining things is the storage of unhealthy thoughts or words. You've probably encountered many people who didn't value you or your dreams that much and they most likely didn't care about what they said to you. Harboring these words today will destroy your chance to ever arrive at greatness. Get rid of them. I'm sure for some that it's easier said than done, but it must be at the top of your priorities.

How much of your delay in producing is because of what someone said? How much of it is because of what someone did or didn't do? It'll amaze you how much we don't move forward because of the weight we carry inside.

Experiencing wipe out is the act of clearing out damaging materials of any kind. Disconnecting from relationships that aren't pushing you forward and making the choice to move forward beyond those things to pursue something greater.

Can you imagine the hidden potential hat will be unlocked as you get out of the box of disappointment and discouragement by choosing to step out on what you know is real? Get rid of the junk today.

Putting the Work In

The only real difference between having an imagination and the reality of it is WORK. Most dreams, visions, or personal aspirations can become tangible if the correct amount of effort is placed into it. I hear a lot of conversations about how things aren't working right for some people or how much time it's taking for individuals to actually achieve their goals. But the truth is that many people only daydream. We spend tons of time working in our heads and not really putting our hands to work towards them in everyday life.

There's no such thing as effortless success. You can sit, hoping and praying and without work nothing is ever going to happen for you. You have a responsibility not only to think it or speak it but also to act on it.

To place an effort towards something is to make a serious attempt towards it. As you've gone through this book and read through the lessons and points, what are some of the goals that you have put serious efforts towards? There can't be any room in your mind that you can ever arrive at any place of success without some form of energy coming out of you towards it. You are the element that makes your dreams come true. No one else holds that right but you. The product seen is in direct relation to the amount of energy you place towards it. A poor-quality product is the result of poor energy when making it.

Always remember that to experience the joy of the harvest, you also have to enjoy the burden of putting the work in to get there. Refuse to let the weight of the work get you off course. Stay strong! Keep working.

Develop Support Systems

I love to talk about support systems because they are vital to the growth and development of our visions. I often look at the scaffolding that surrounds new construction. It fascinates me to see a building being erected inside of it. The scaffolding supports the crew while holding the materials they need to complete it without coming down every time they require something. How many times have you been forced to stop working because the support necessary wasn't in place? I want to give you a few pointers that might help you to never have to come down again.

As you build towards greatness, you will always need divine support systems. These aren't the people who simply come to watch the game and then leave you on the field. These are individuals who are invested in seeing you grow and be successful. I know that we can sometimes get so tired of giving chances and getting disappointed, but I do believe that there are individuals who are assigned to your vision and they want to see you do it. Do you know who those individuals are yet? If not, let's keep reading.

There's a difference between encouragement and support. Your life sometimes is filled with many encouragers. These are individuals who will call, text and email to communicate their support of what you're doing and working towards. While we all need encouragers, when the work begins, you'll need supporters.

Supporters are those who not only encourage you to do the good job but who also show up to help you do the good job. You need them both. What you are doing is great and will take the reinforcement of individuals who just want to see you accomplish what's in your heart.

Scope out those whom you can really count on. Don't be distracted if the audience leaves when the game is getting rough. Choose rather to focus on the individuals who are still in the dugout waiting on the chance to help you win the game and finish strong.

Here's some questions to help you evaluate your support system:

- Who can I really depend on?
- Who are my encouragers and supporters?
- Who are the individuals that I can look to for advice and information?
- Who are the people that I know for sure only want to see me succeed?

- Who are my investors? Who are those individuals who are willing to invest in what I believe in?

Believe it or not. The major victories that will occur in your life will not come from those who are cheering in the stands, but rather from those who are glad to support you behind the scenes. Some people will only use your cause as a way out of what they may be experiencing personally. After they accomplish their goal, they're gone, and you're left wondering why. Your success now becomes their strife.

Recognize early those who are with you for who you are genuinely and not only for what they can benefit from as you work towards your goals. Once you start setting standards for these types of relationships, it will be easy to move forward and gain the necessary momentum needed.

Lastly, most of us won't be able to develop strong support systems until we begin the process of eliminating conflicting partnerships. Conflicting partnerships are those that have nothing to do with your current efforts or those that are not sincere in their support for you. Don't ever assume that everyone who shows up to help is 100% invested in seeing you successful. Sometimes individuals help only to receive a portion of the rewards to benefit their chosen ventures.

In addition, don't assume that your last partners were your greatest partners. If they are gone, don't overreact thinking that you can't build or survive without them. Could it be that they had to be removed to make room for more viable partners? Continue to make room in your heart for fresh opportunities for change. As your vision expands so will your need for fresh innovation and support. Don't shut down because of weakening support.

Hire Yourself

I want you to begin the process of getting more involved in your dreams. We often look for others to spearhead the process and do most of the work but becoming great will take your work as well as the support you have in place. Against popular opinion, there is no such thing as the abracadabra vision. You just don't see it today and enjoy it tomorrow without working for it. Now, I'm sure we all wished it worked that way in most cases, but it doesn't.

You must always hire yourself first in the same vision that you want others to participate in. As they see you work, it'll become more exciting to those that you've shared it with. No one wants to join a team where the captain isn't excited. Your excitement is demonstrated to others through your commitment to work for what you believe in.

If you are to ever build consistently, there must be an attitude of making your own way through your intention and willingness to work FIRST. Here are four intentions that should be a part of your success plan:

1. Intend to build.
2. Intend to prepare.
3. Intend sacrifice resources.
4. Intend to finish.

Get rid of the start and stop mentality

There are so many things in life that we start and stop. Therefore, we never develop the mindset of finishing anything. If you are to ever achieve true greatness in life, you'll have to make it a habit to always finish what you start.

Take the time to carve out ways that will help you complete tasks and achieve goals. Place consistent effort behind every desire, dream, and vision until it's not only seen, but also enjoyed. Remember this. Your vision should not only consist of a lifelong journey of work and no enjoyment. You are supposed to not only enjoy what you do but also what it produces.

Your dream in its maximum potential is going to be so worth the work. But you've got to know this for yourself. It's the lack of energy towards something that generally tells the true story of what is occurring in your heart and mind concerning a project or plan. Whenever you lack the energy to work on dream building, it is usually an internal indication that you may not see the full picture yet. Don't play it off by saying that you're too busy or can't find the time. Have you ever heard the saying, "Where there's a will, there's a way"? This is an absolutely true statement. Whenever something is divinely a part of you, there's nothing that can come to stop you from experiencing it. Evaluate your heart to determine whether what you're seeing is a true vision or just a pipe dream that can be tossed to make room for a wiser investment.

FOCUS ON THE FINISH

We've now come to the end of what I believe has been a remarkable journey of reflection and encouragement for you.

In life, our eyes will be drawn to so many areas. It seems like everything wants our attention and we're getting delayed at every stage. We'll see a lot of things and experience more than what we would like. But the goal is to always stay focused on what you know is your reality.

Try not to explain what has no definition yet. There will be times that you won't be able to communicate to others what you only know as a feeling or sense of a better day. Don't allow the definition of what would help someone else understand it limit you. Enjoy the pursuit of watching it expand within you every day.

Stay away from negative sources. Don't be fooled out of a great thing by pausing its development to pursue discouraging words, unhealthy relationships, or damaging distractions. Choose today to continue working on something by avoiding the distractions that come while building something great. Let's make it happen. We can do this together!

What would happen if you started to view the destination you have in mind as only the starting point? Don't things look that much better now? You've got the point. Now it's time to work!

Aaron J. Mobley, Jr.

Made in the USA
Columbia, SC
29 September 2022

67781991R00085